Manly
(an Adult Coloring Book)

D.P. Turoczy

ISBN-13: 978-0-9965499-9-8

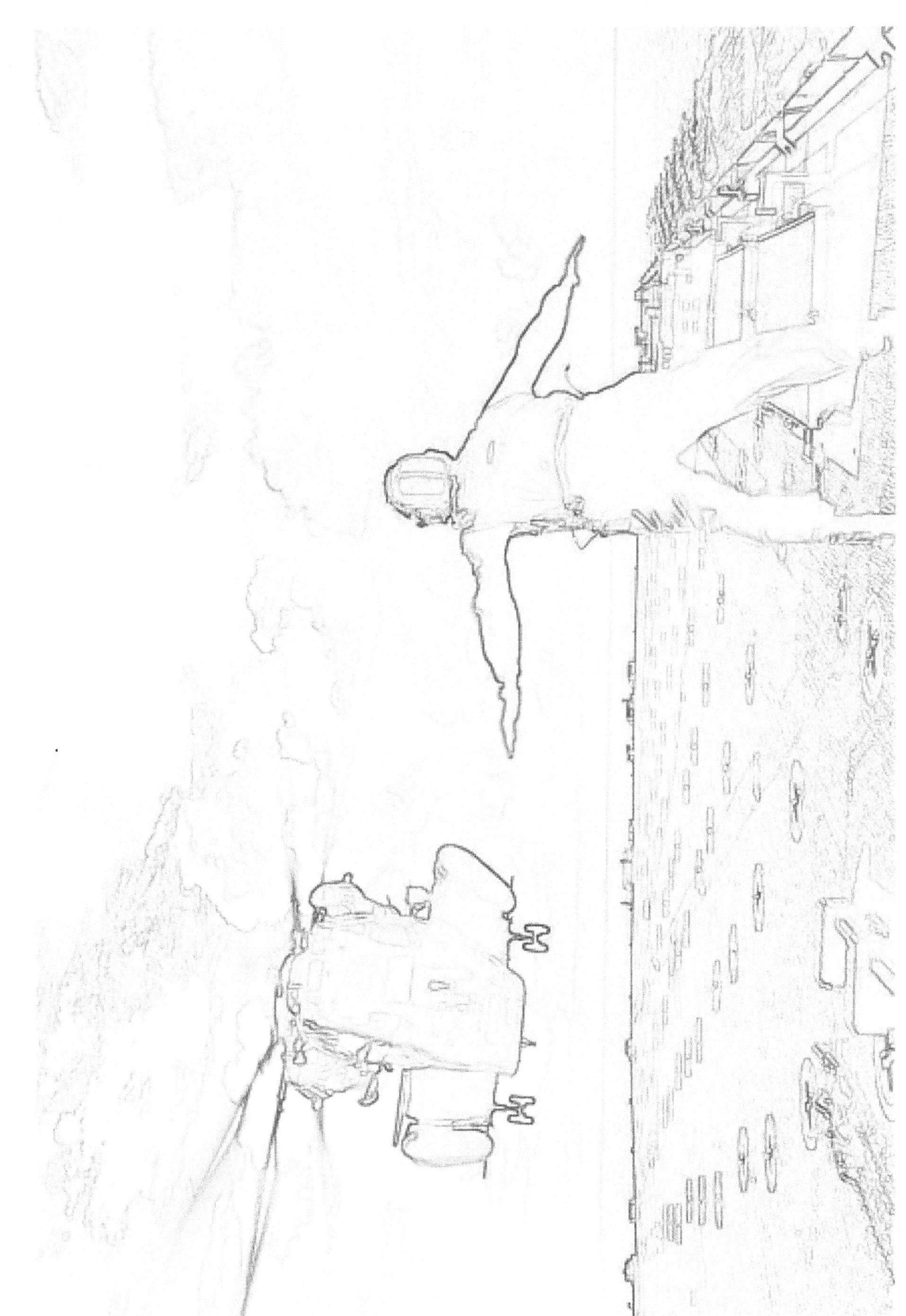

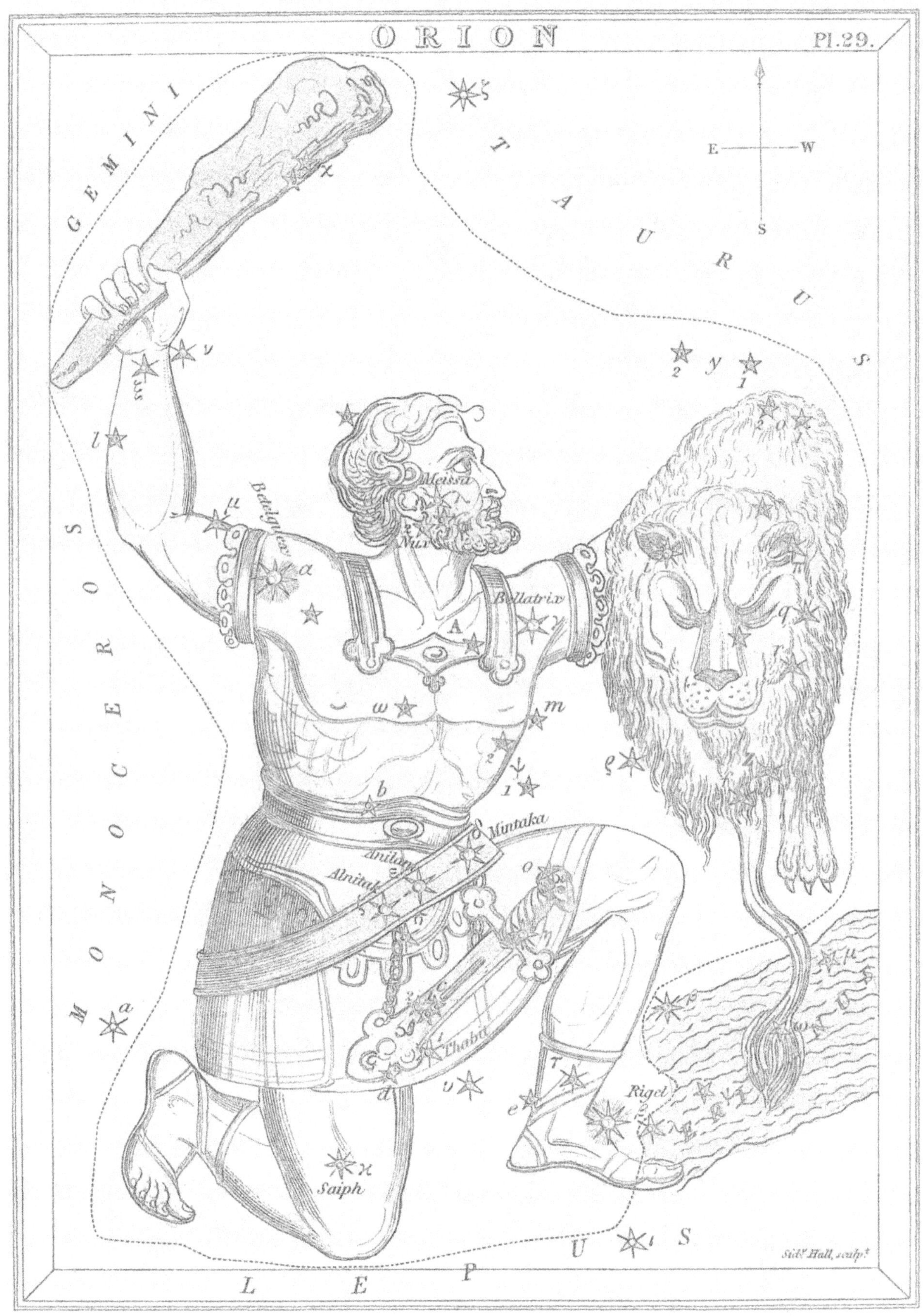
ORION
Pl. 29.
GEMINI
TAURUS
MONOCEROS
LEPUS
E
W
S
Betelgeux
Meissa
Bellatrix
Mintaka
Alnilam
Alnitak
Thabit
Rigel
Saiph
Sidy. Hall, sculp.

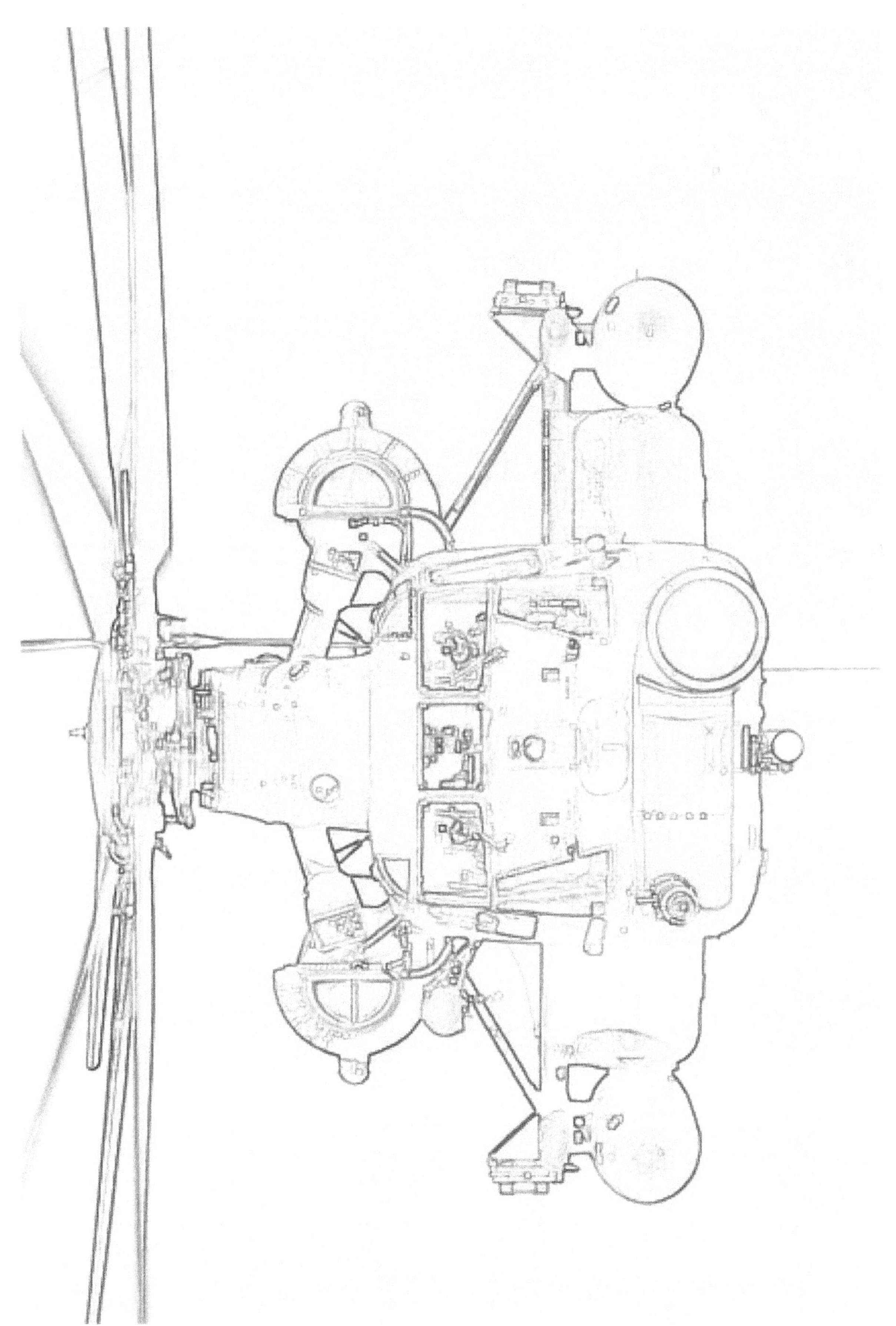

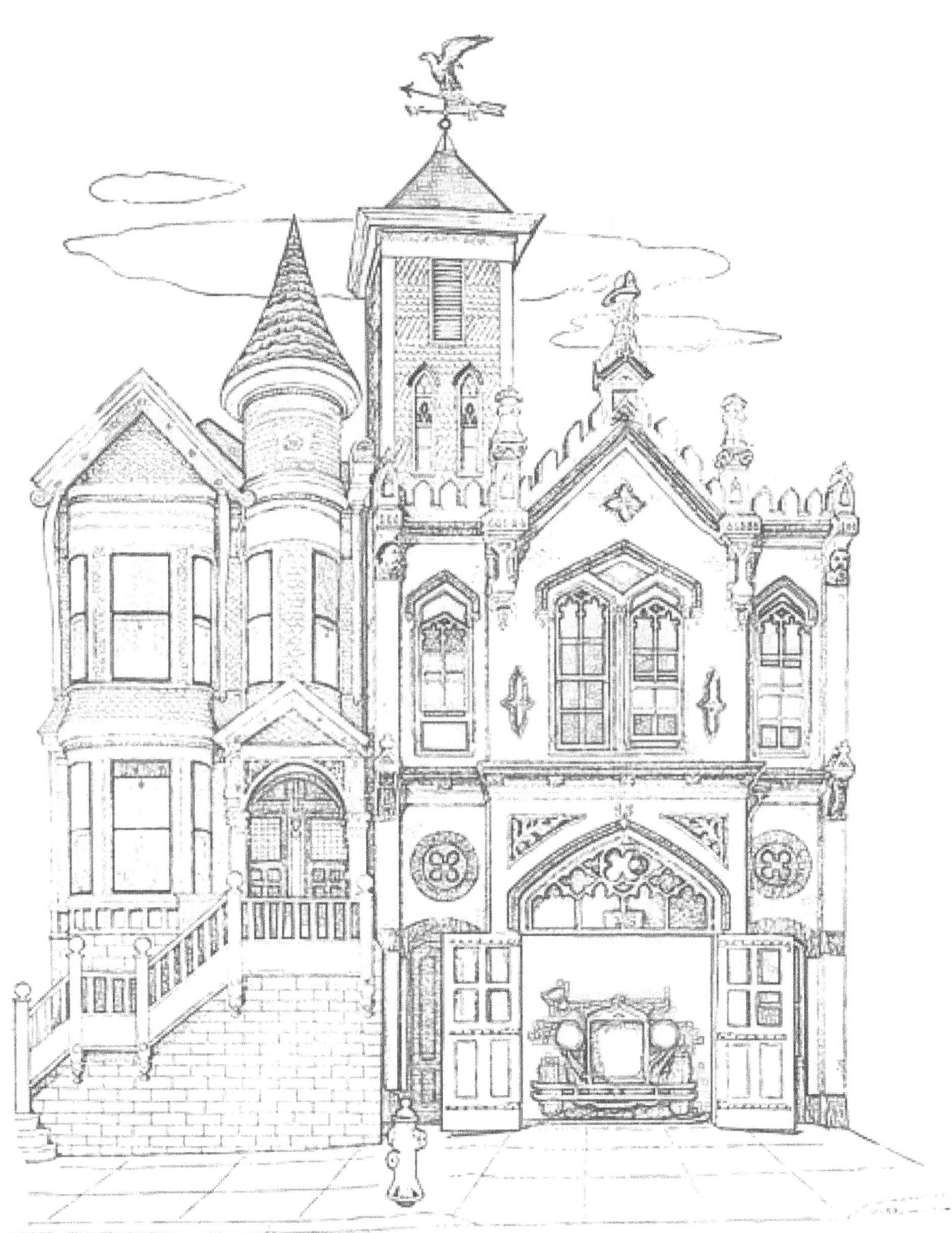

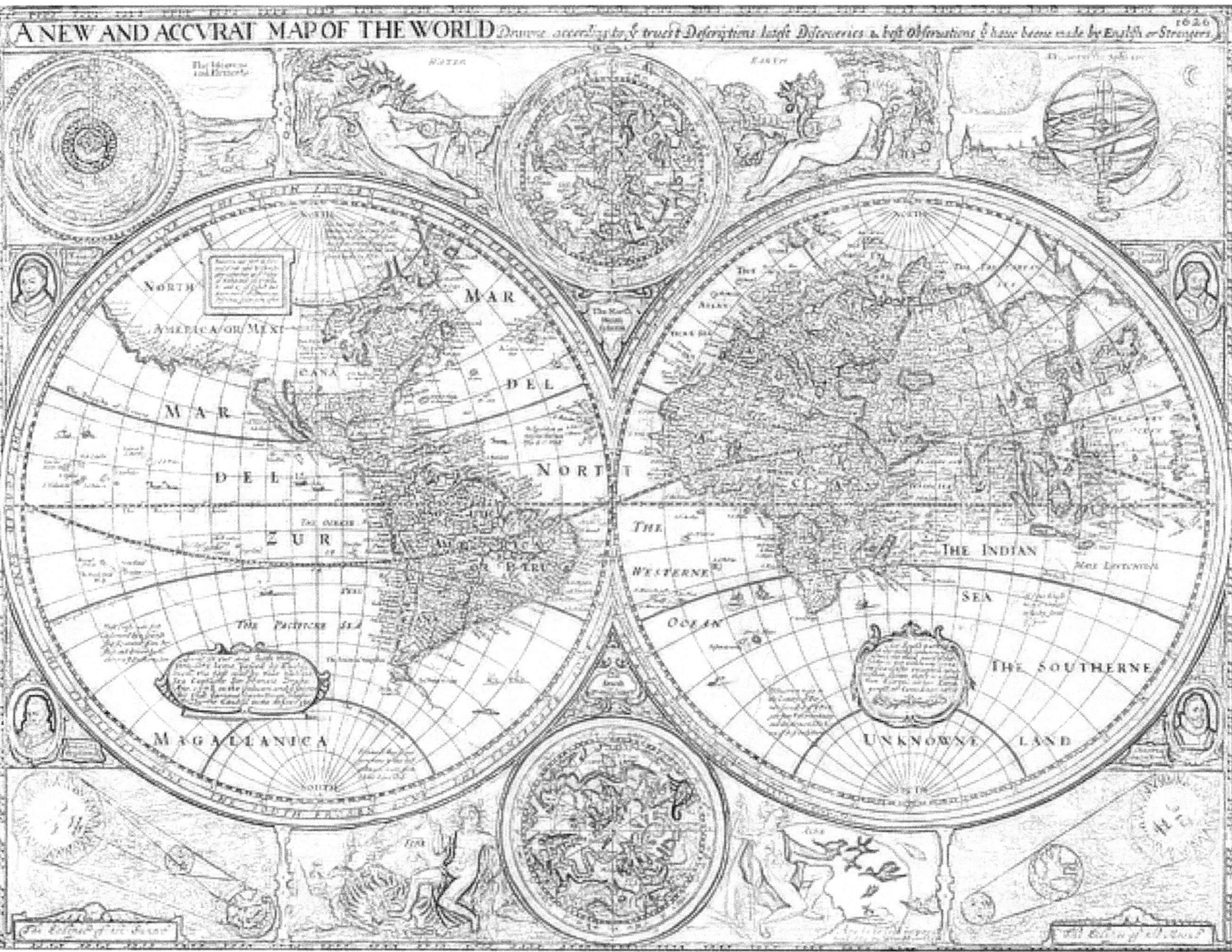

A NEW AND ACCVRAT MAP OF THE WORLD
1626
NORTH AMERICA OR MEXICANA
MAR DEL NORT
MAR DEL ZUR
THE PACIFICKE SEA
MAGALLANICA
THE WESTERNE OCEAN
THE INDIAN SEA
THE SOUTHERNE UNKNOWNE LAND

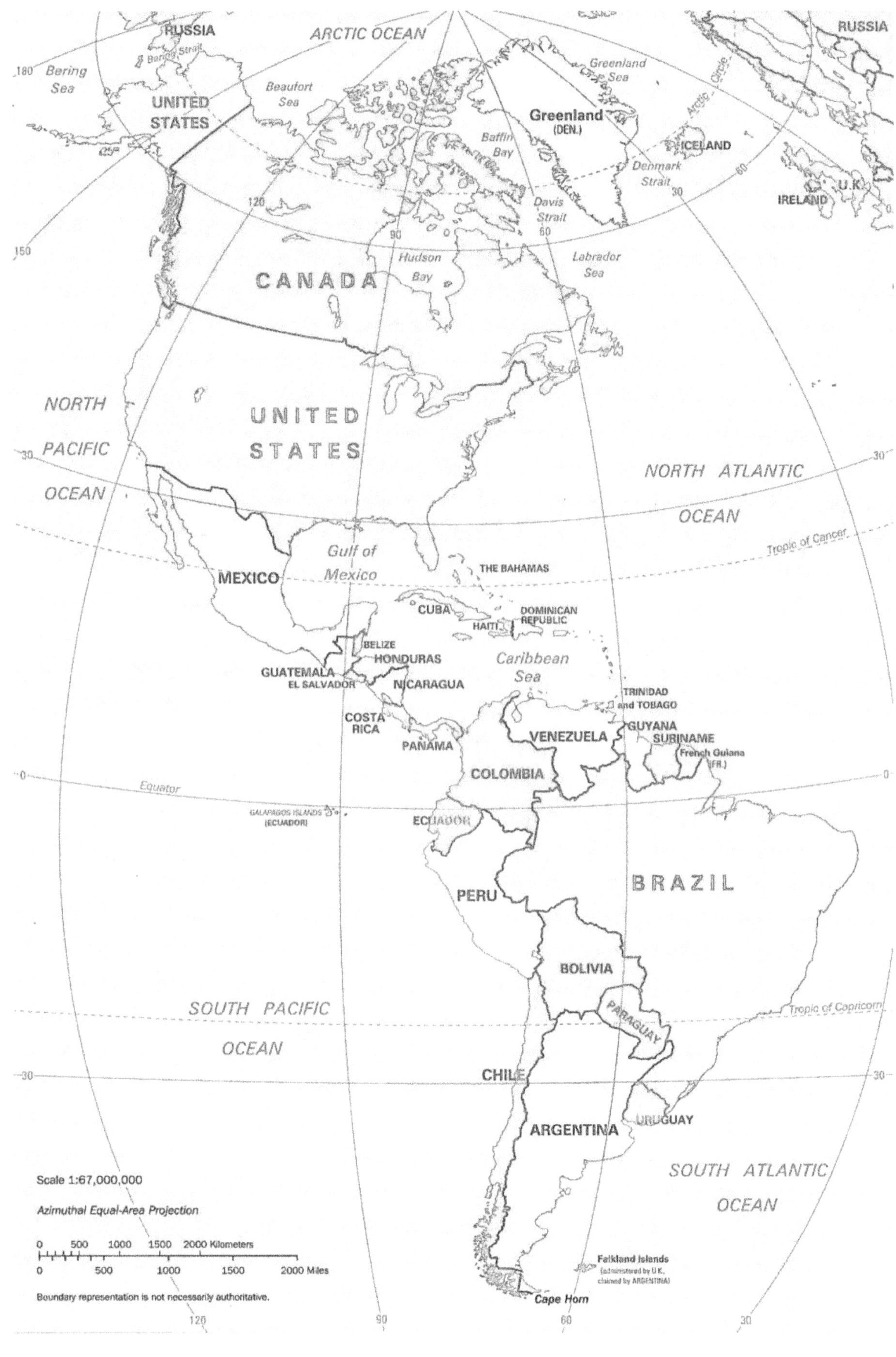

RUSSIA
ARCTIC OCEAN
Bering Strait
Bering Sea
UNITED STATES
Beaufort Sea
Greenland Sea
Greenland (DEN.)
Arctic Circle
ICELAND
Baffin Bay
Denmark Strait
U.K.
IRELAND
Davis Strait
Hudson Bay
Labrador Sea
CANADA
NORTH PACIFIC OCEAN
UNITED STATES
NORTH ATLANTIC OCEAN
Tropic of Cancer
Gulf of Mexico
MEXICO
THE BAHAMAS
CUBA
DOMINICAN REPUBLIC
HAITI
BELIZE
HONDURAS
Caribbean Sea
GUATEMALA
EL SALVADOR
NICARAGUA
TRINIDAD and TOBAGO
COSTA RICA
PANAMA
VENEZUELA
GUYANA
SURINAME
French Guiana (FR.)
COLOMBIA
Equator
GALAPAGOS ISLANDS (ECUADOR)
ECUADOR
PERU
BRAZIL
BOLIVIA
SOUTH PACIFIC OCEAN
PARAGUAY
Tropic of Capricorn
CHILE
ARGENTINA
URUGUAY
SOUTH ATLANTIC OCEAN
Scale 1:67,000,000
Azimuthal Equal-Area Projection
0 500 1000 1500 2000 Kilometers
0 500 1000 1500 2000 Miles
Boundary representation is not necessarily authoritative.
Falkland Islands (administered by U.K., claimed by ARGENTINA)
Cape Horn

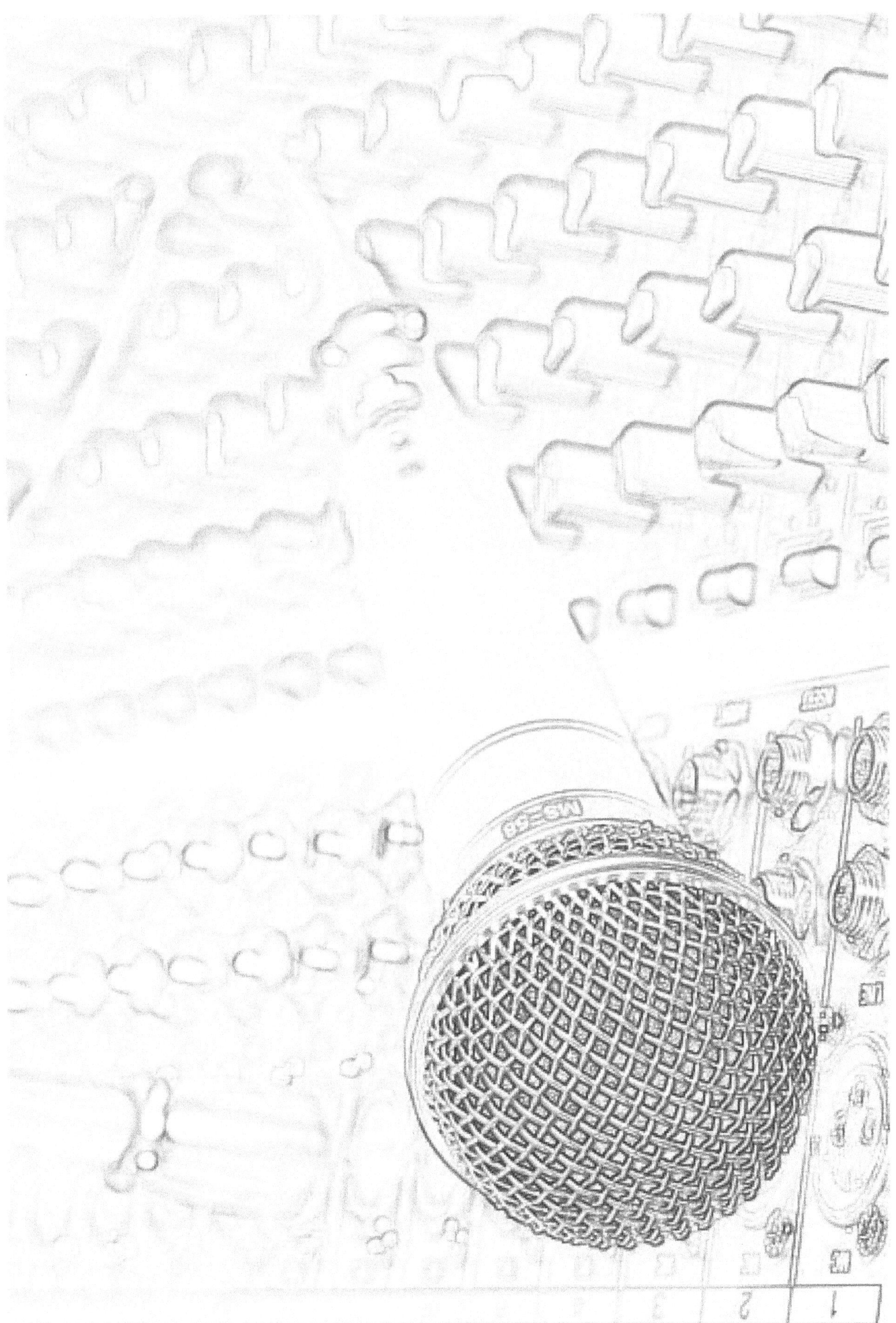

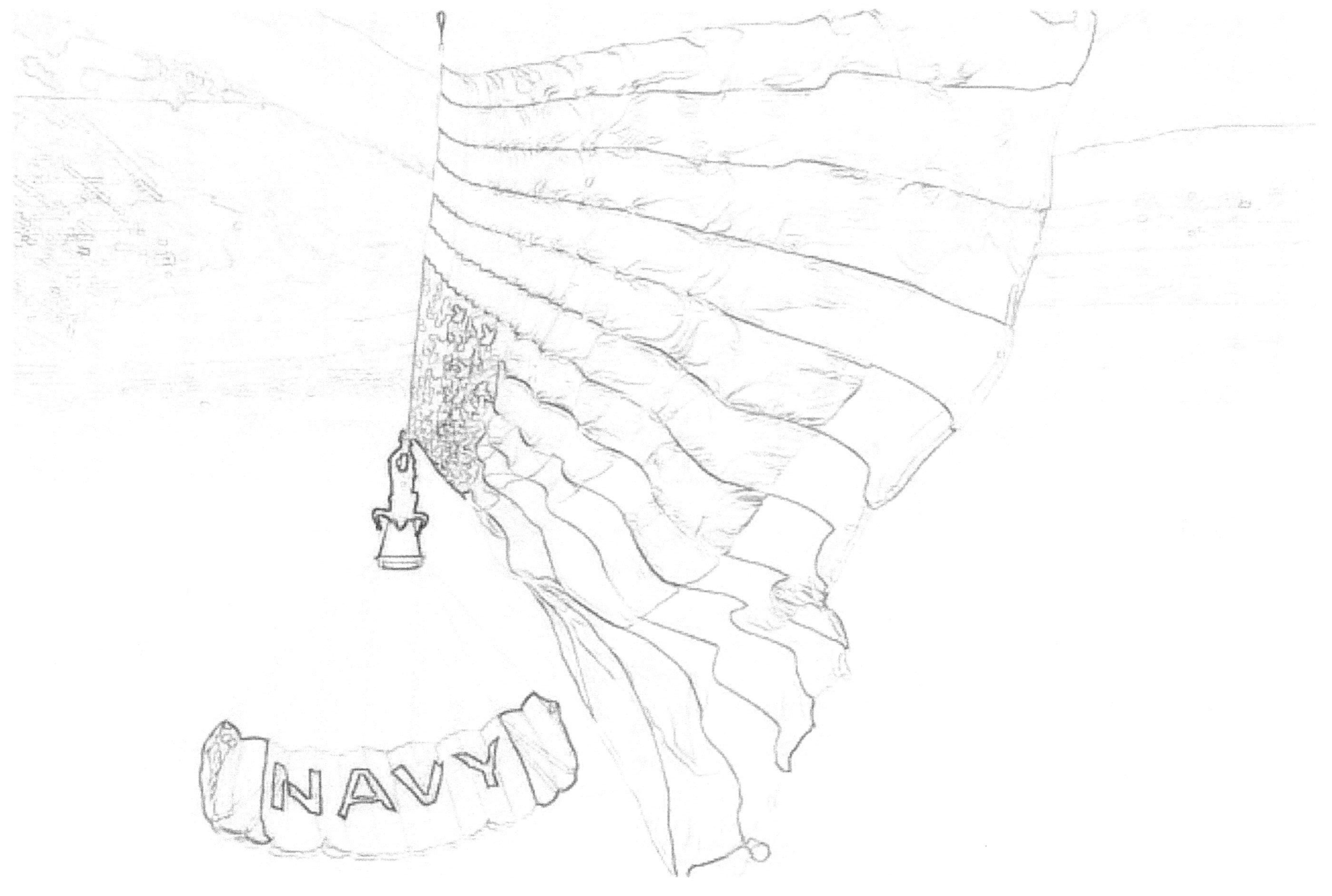
NAVY

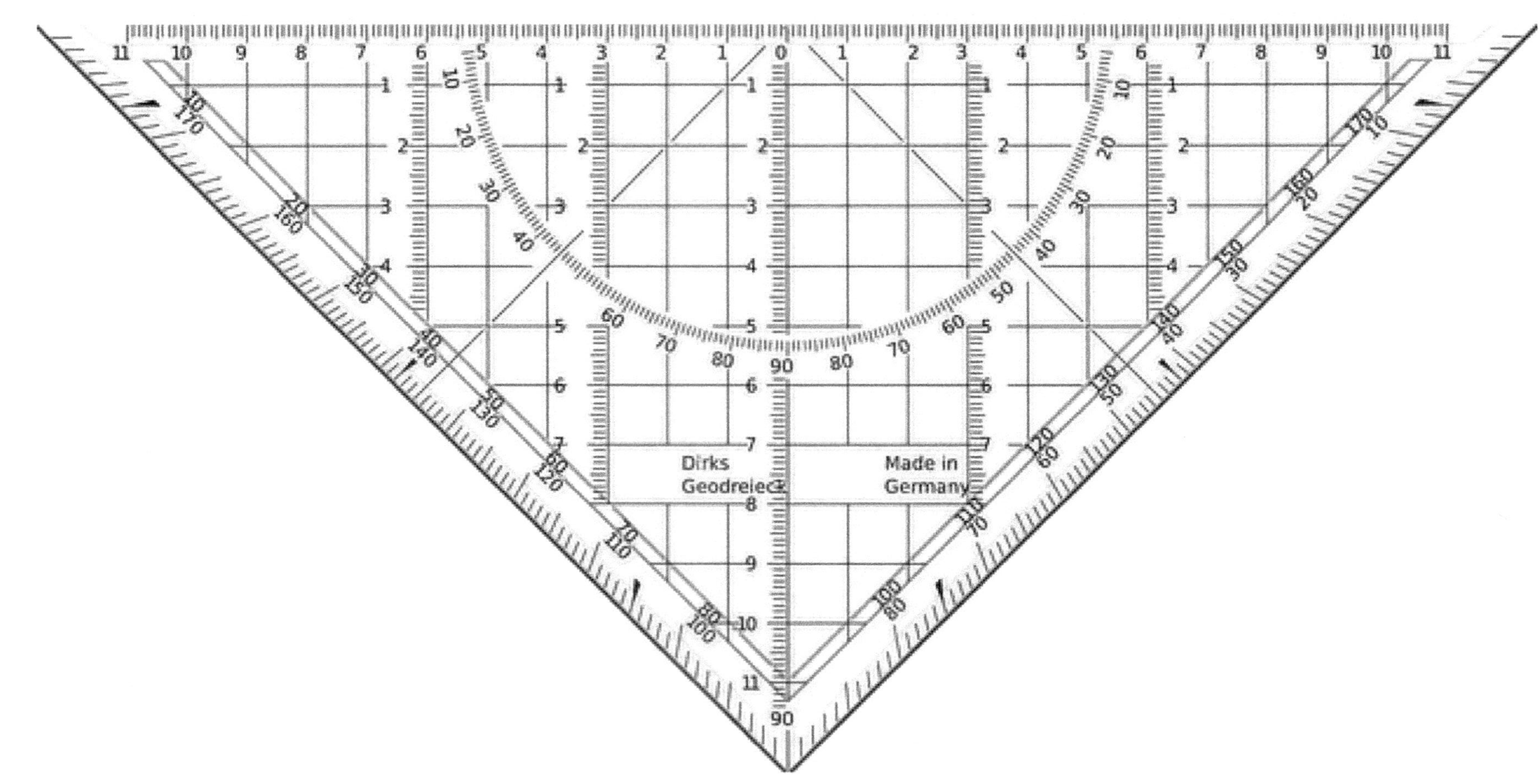
Dirks
Geodreieck
Made in
Germany

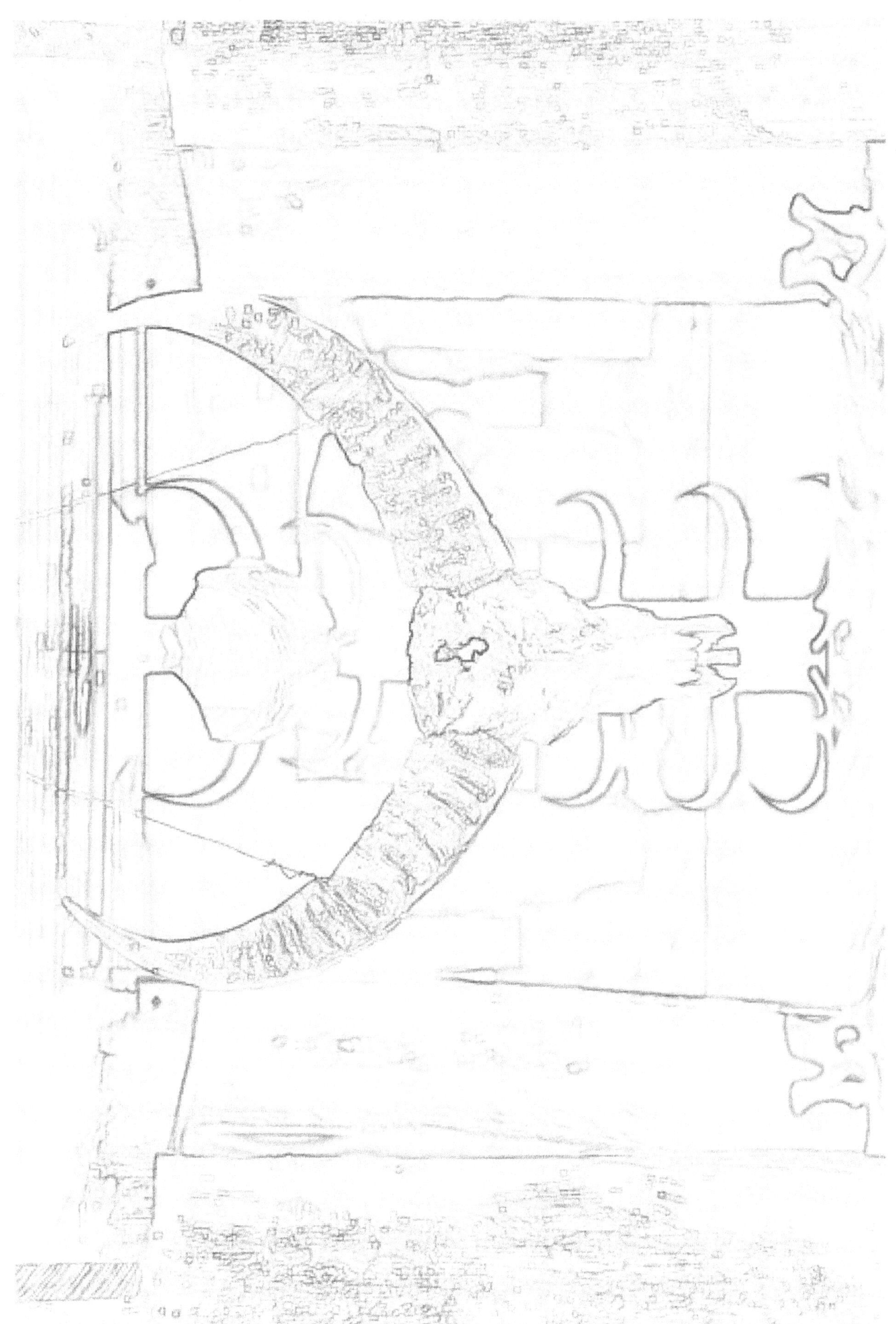

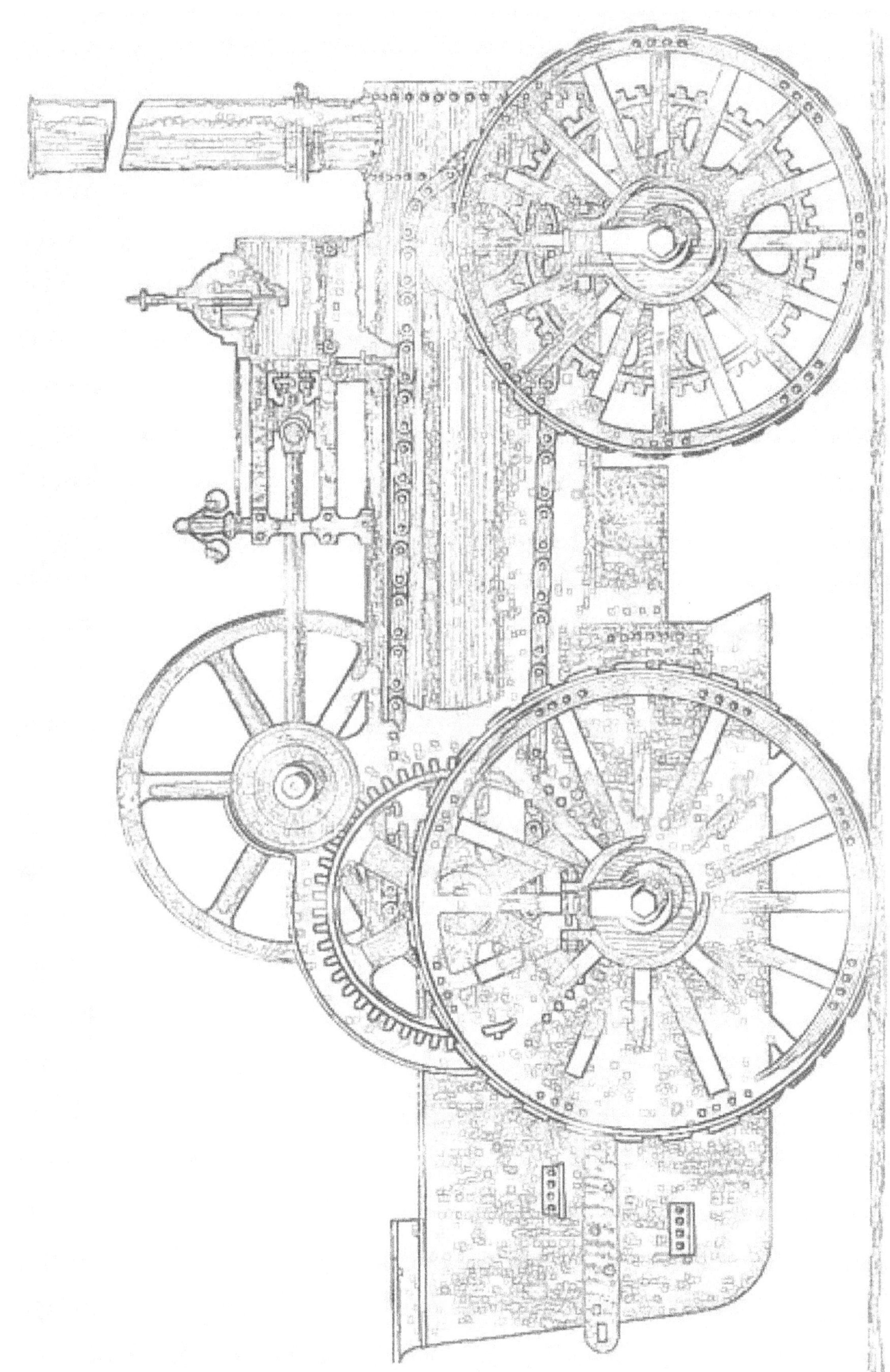

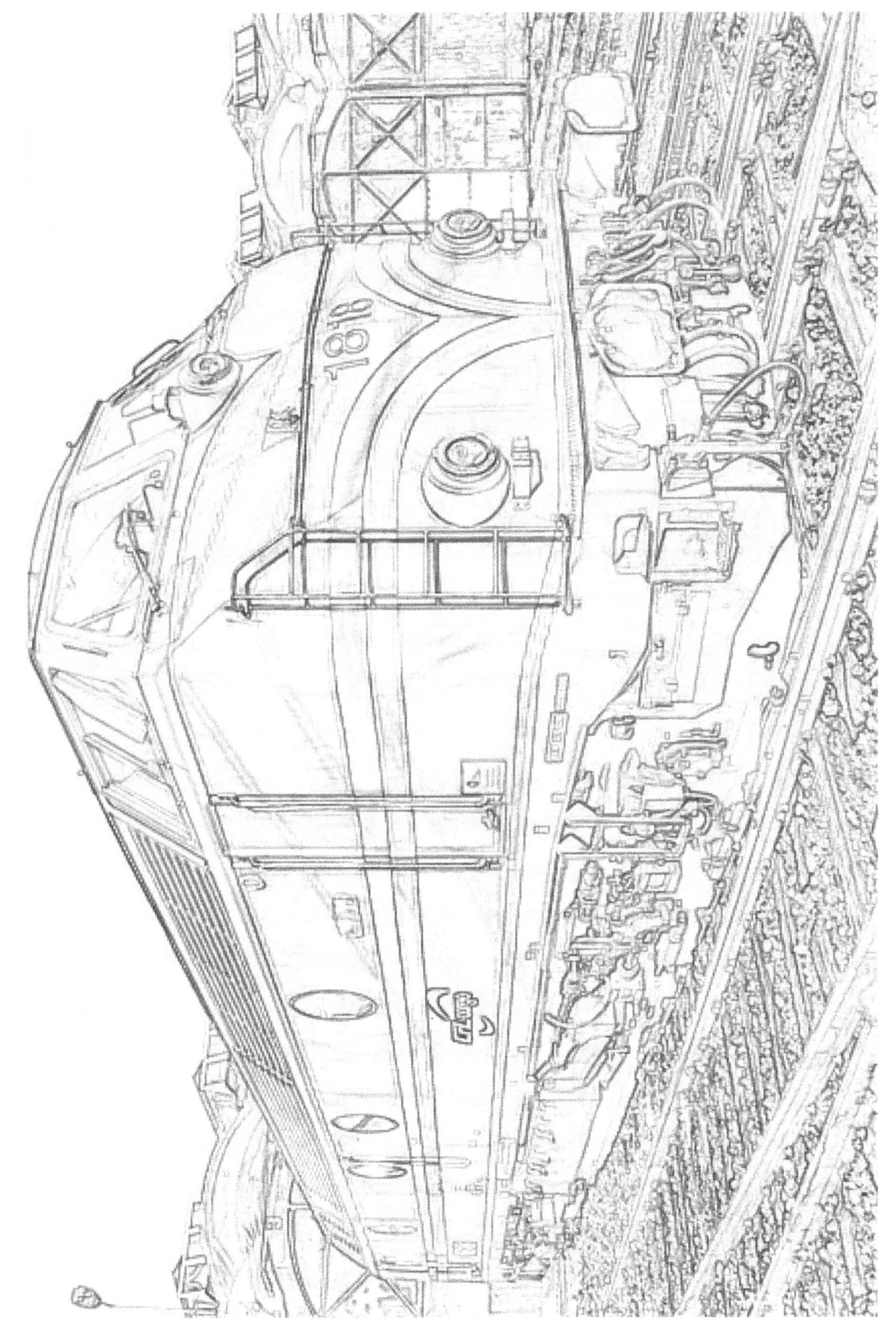

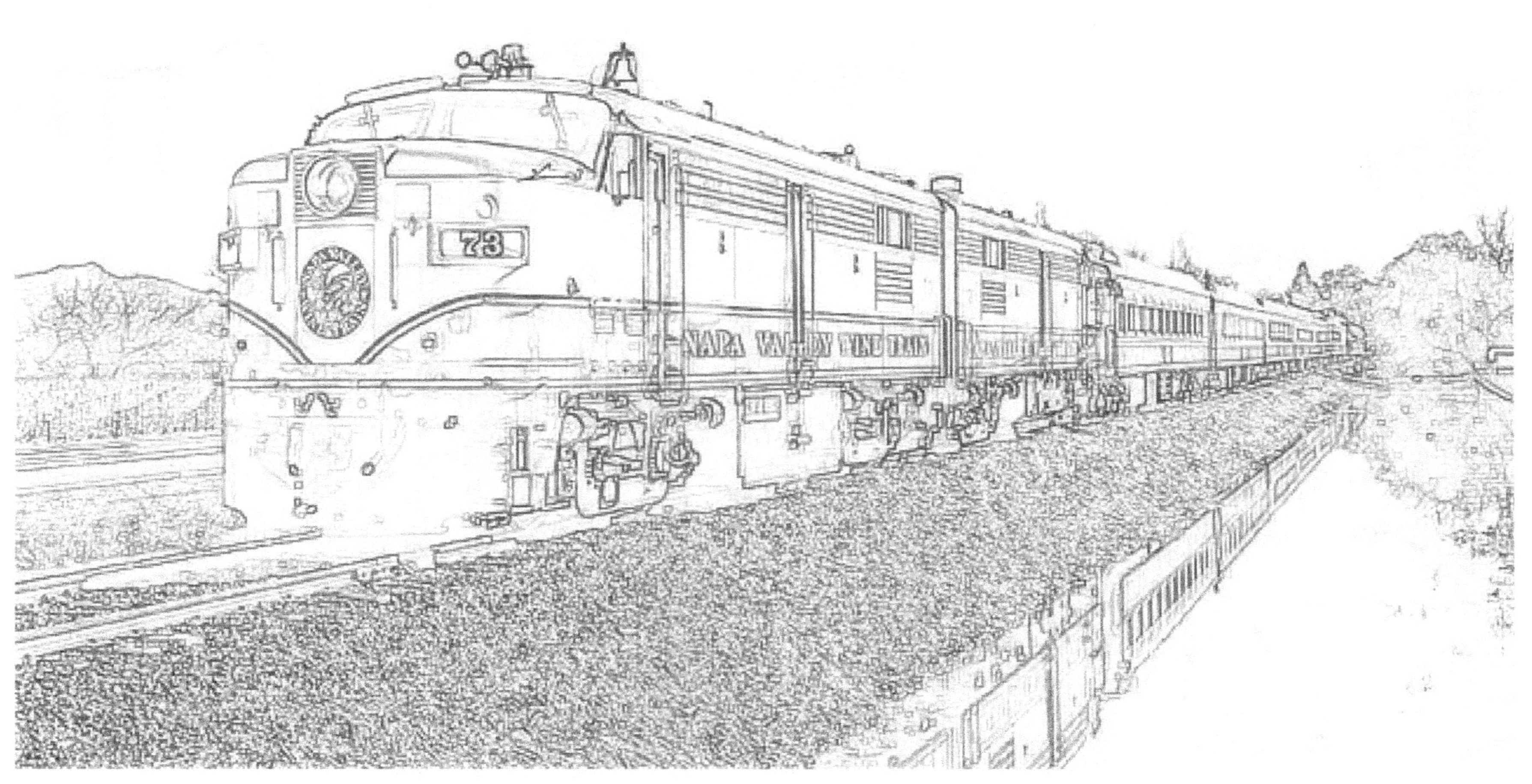
73

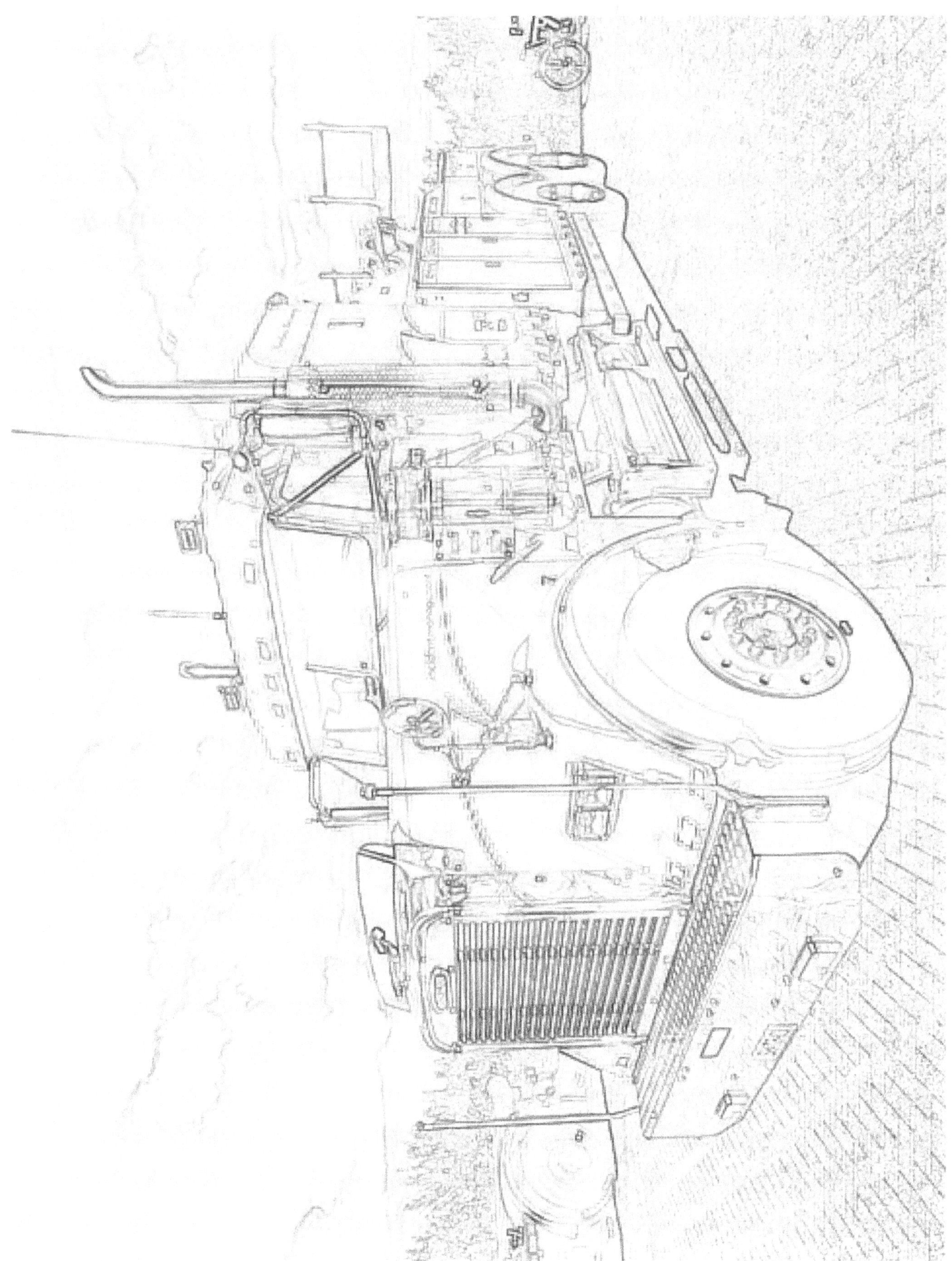

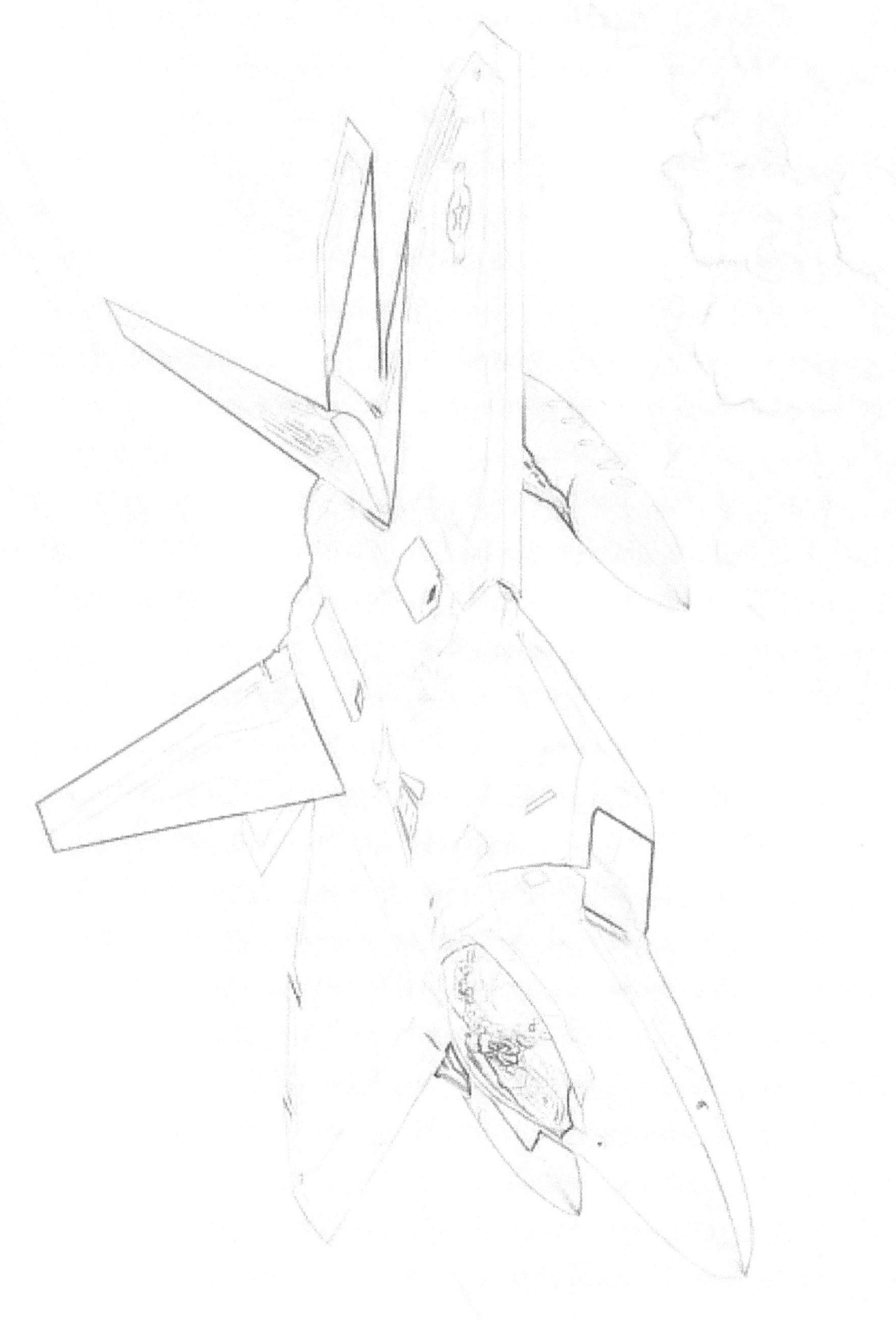

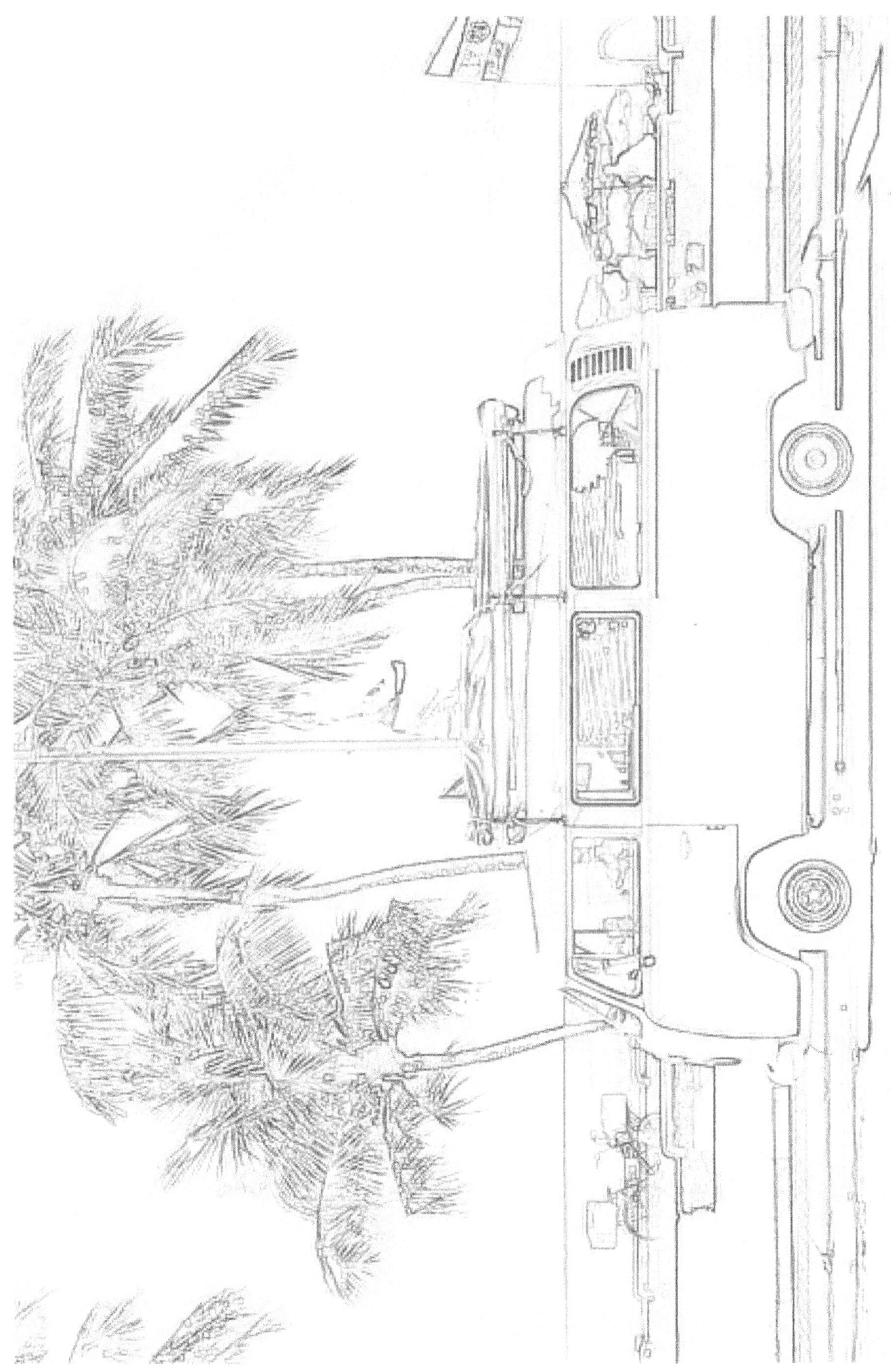

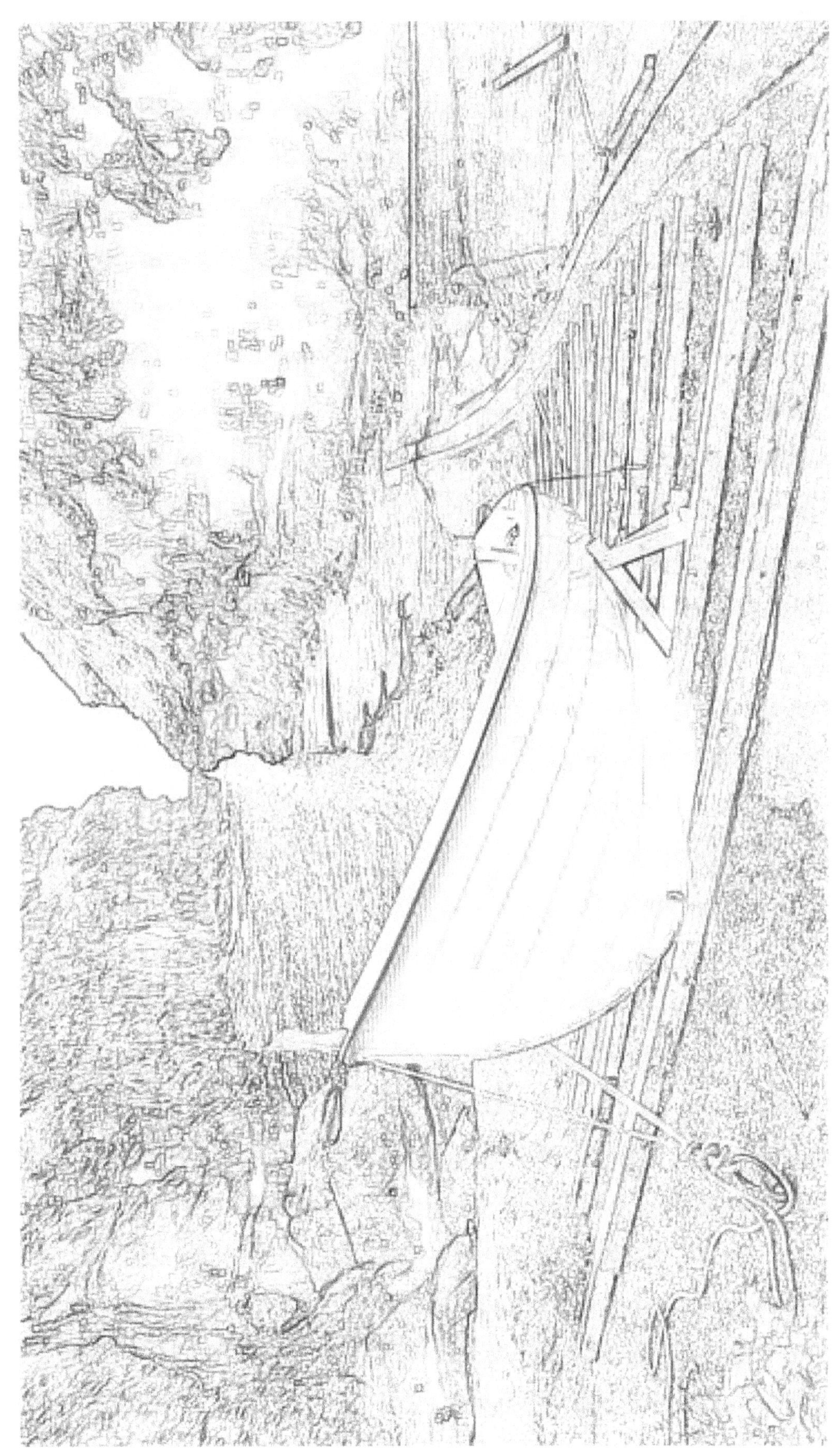

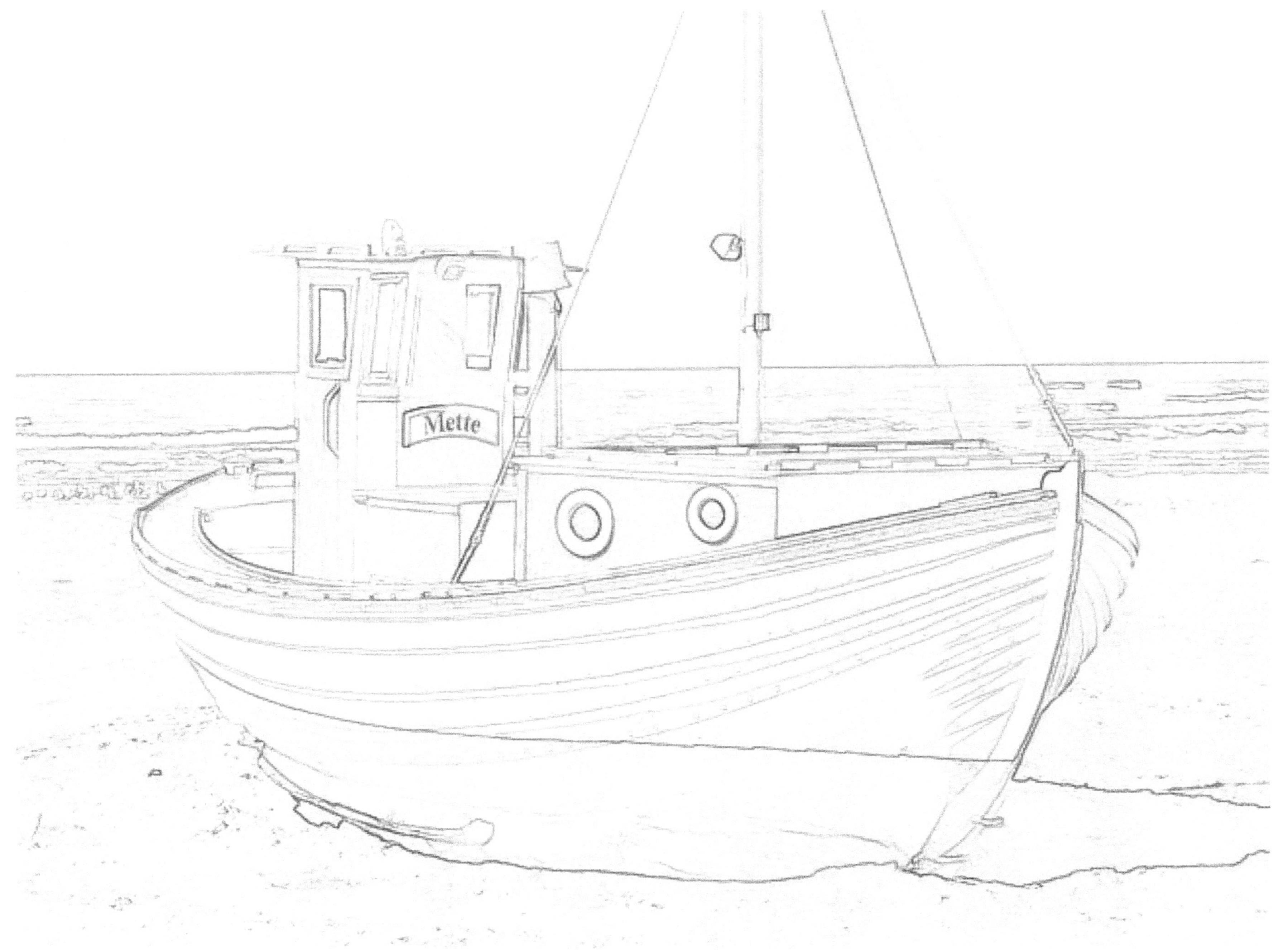
Mette

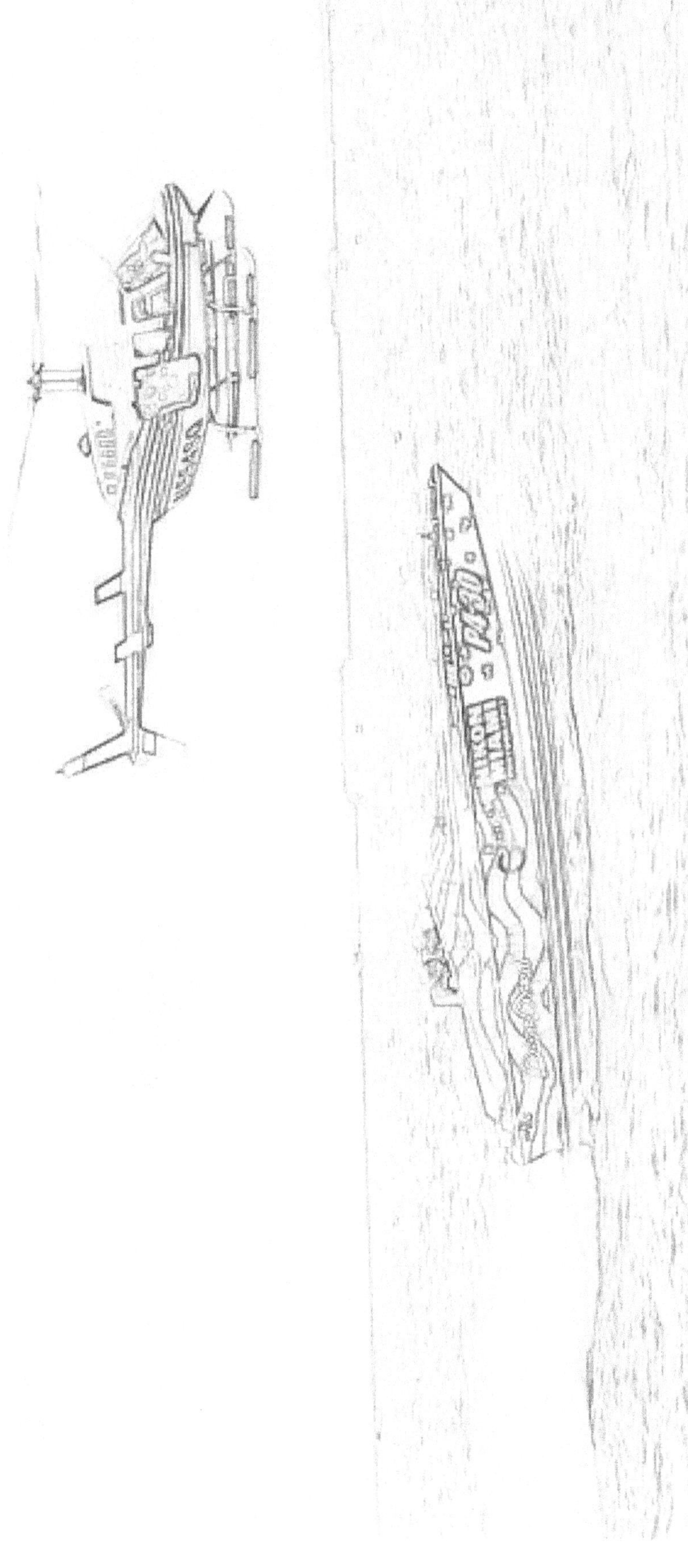

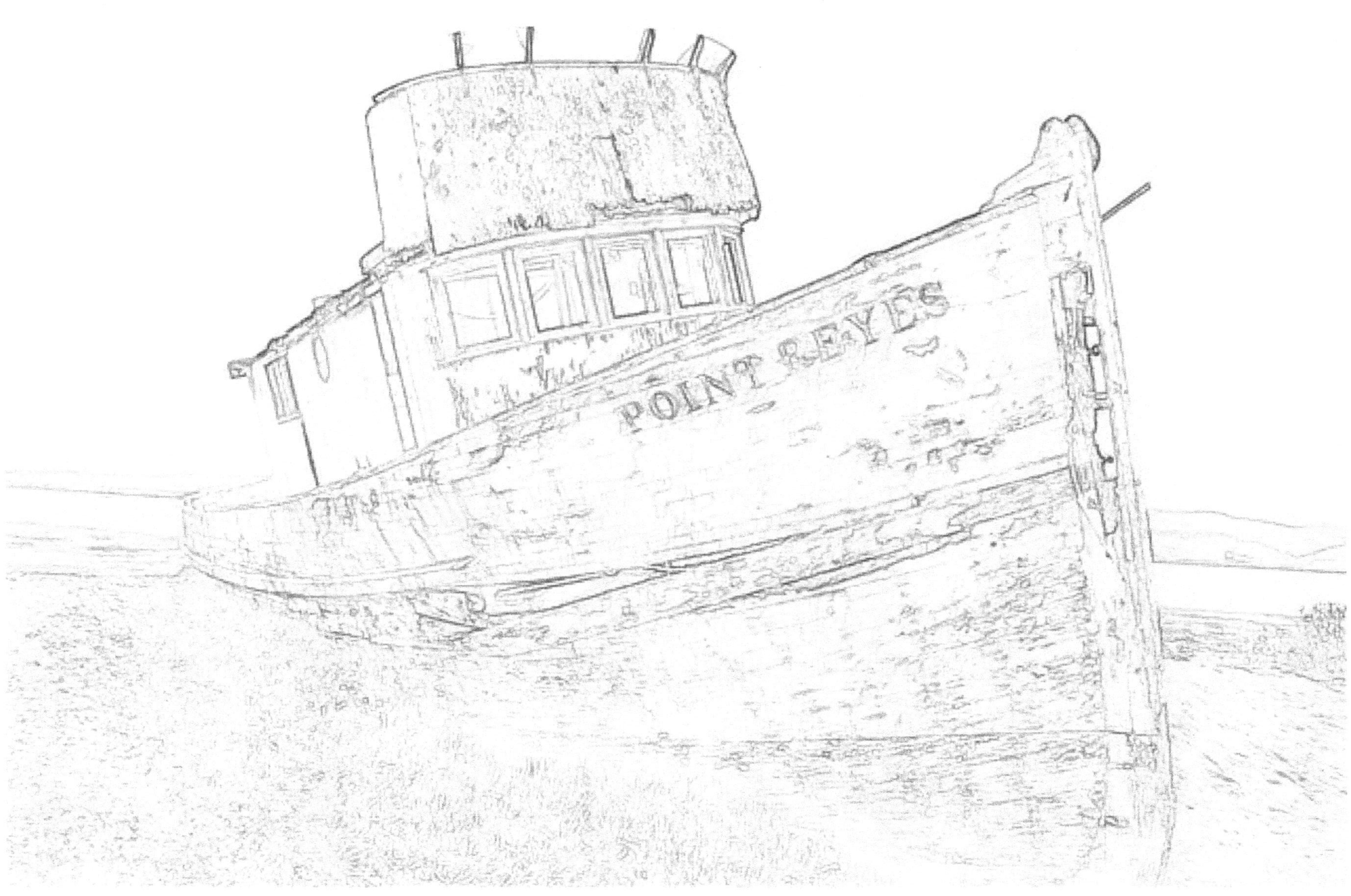
POINT REYES

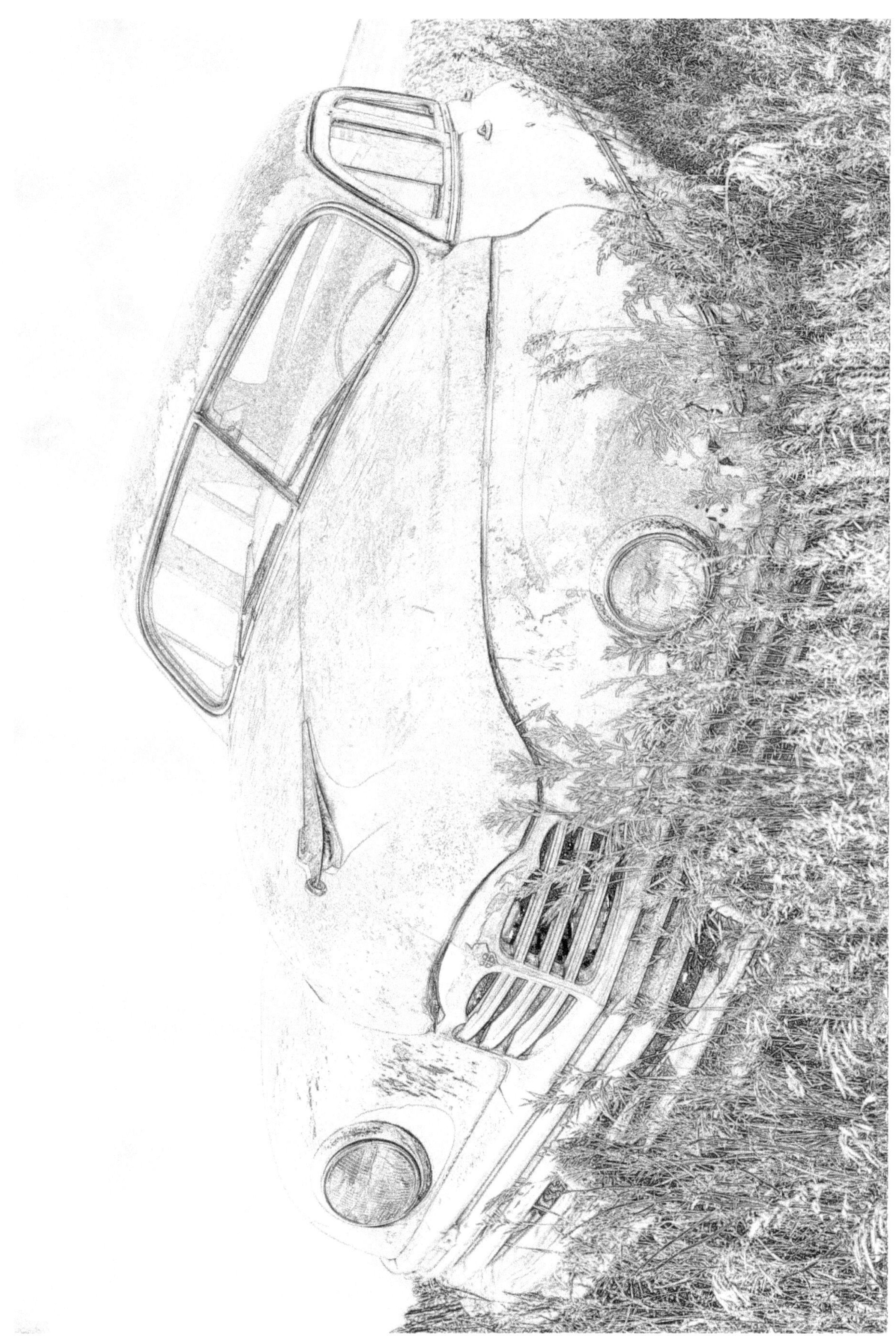

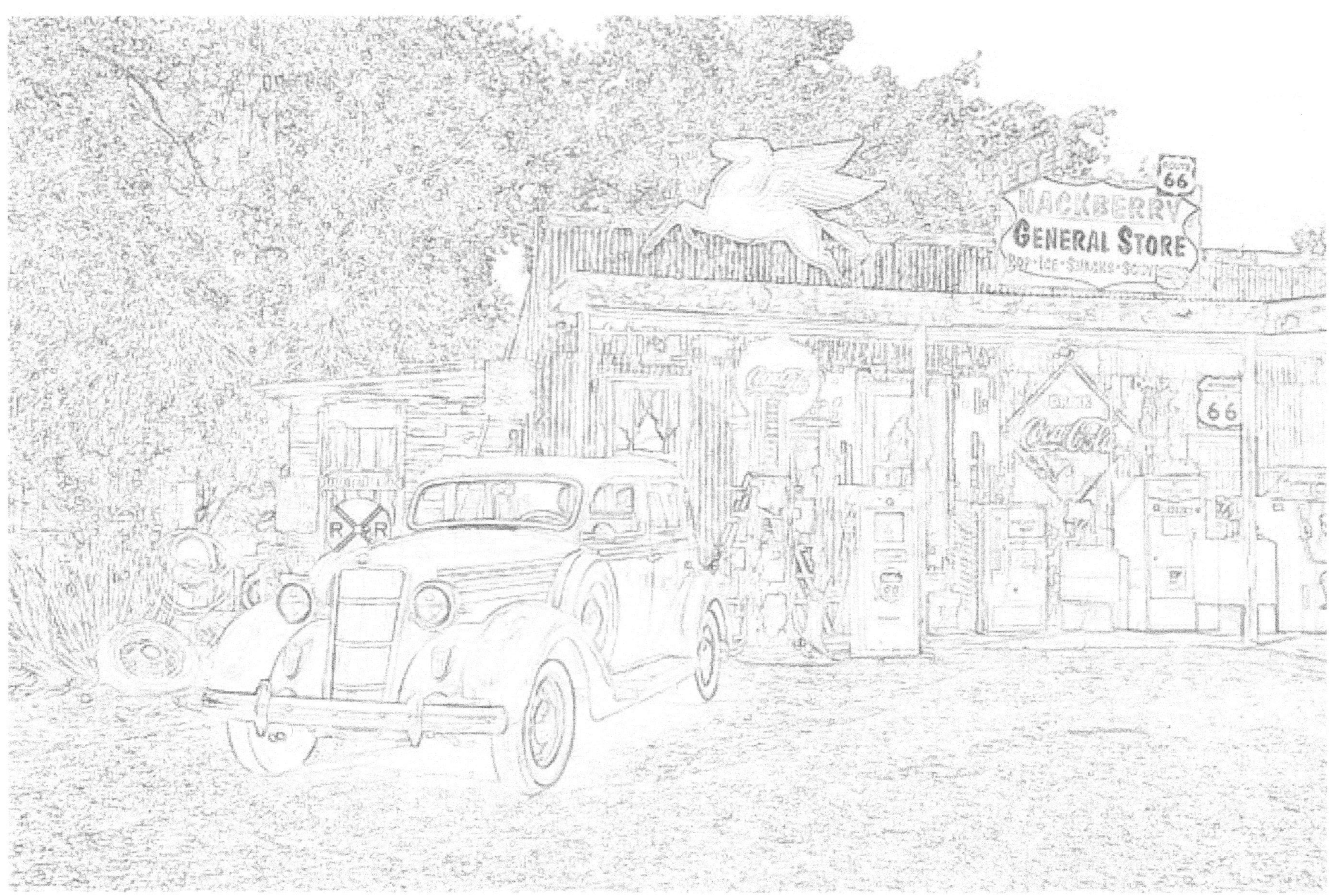
66
GENERAL STORE
66

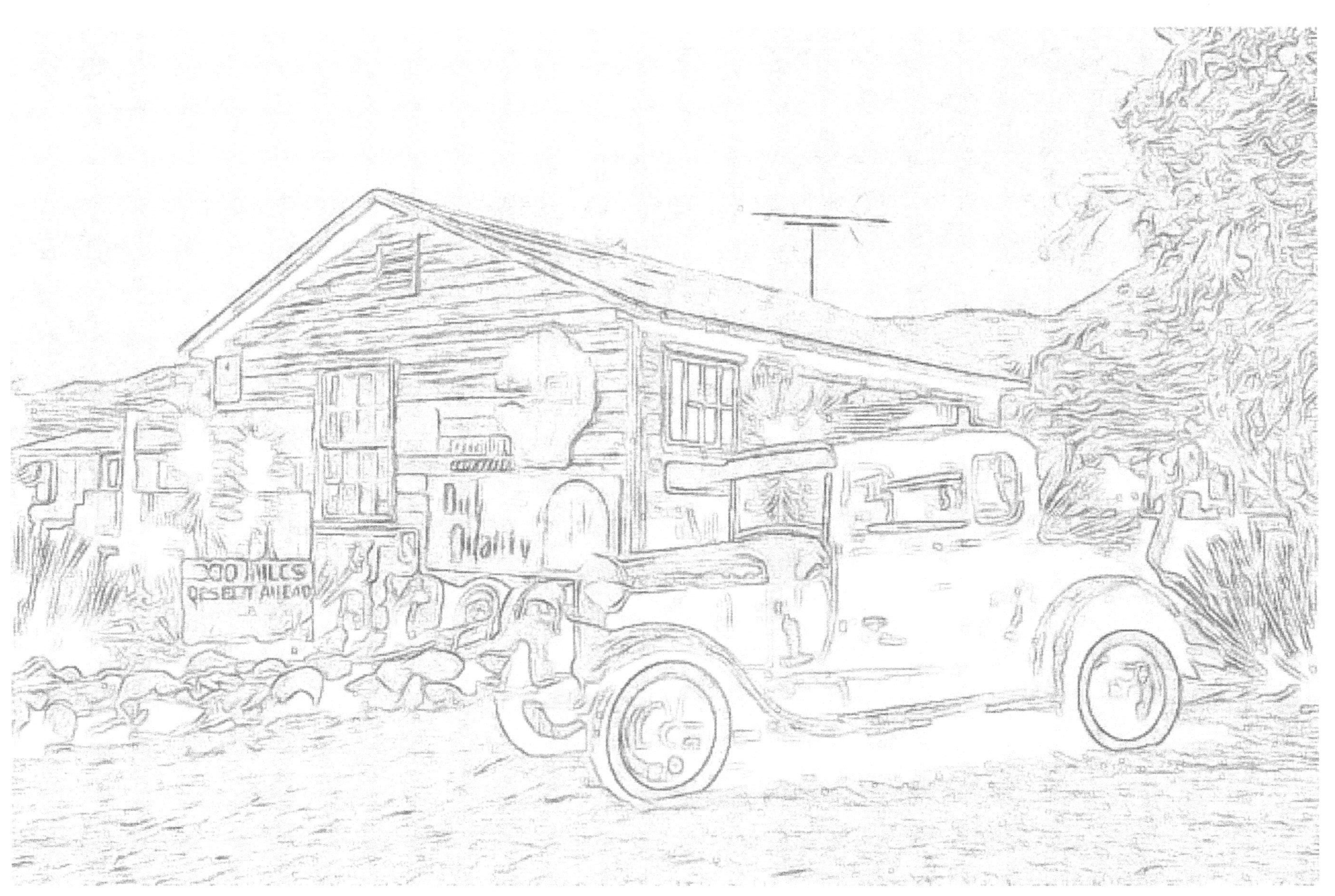

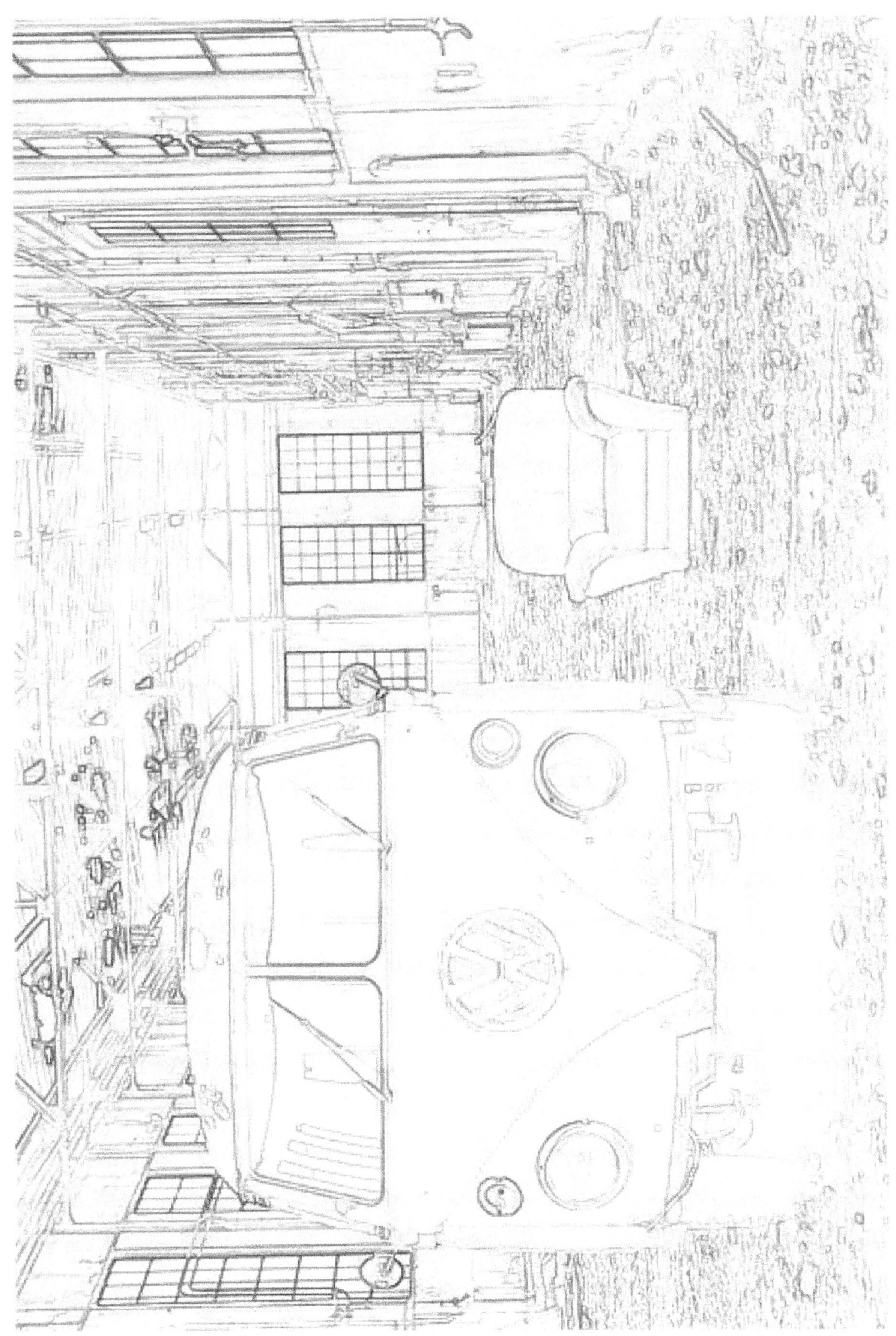

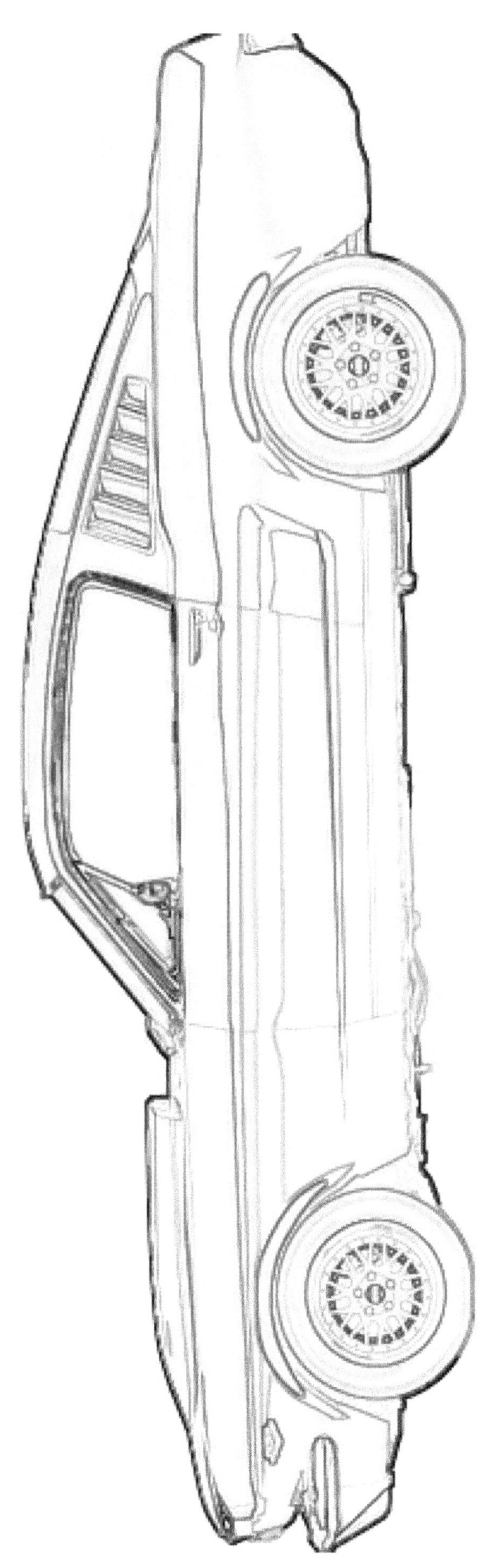

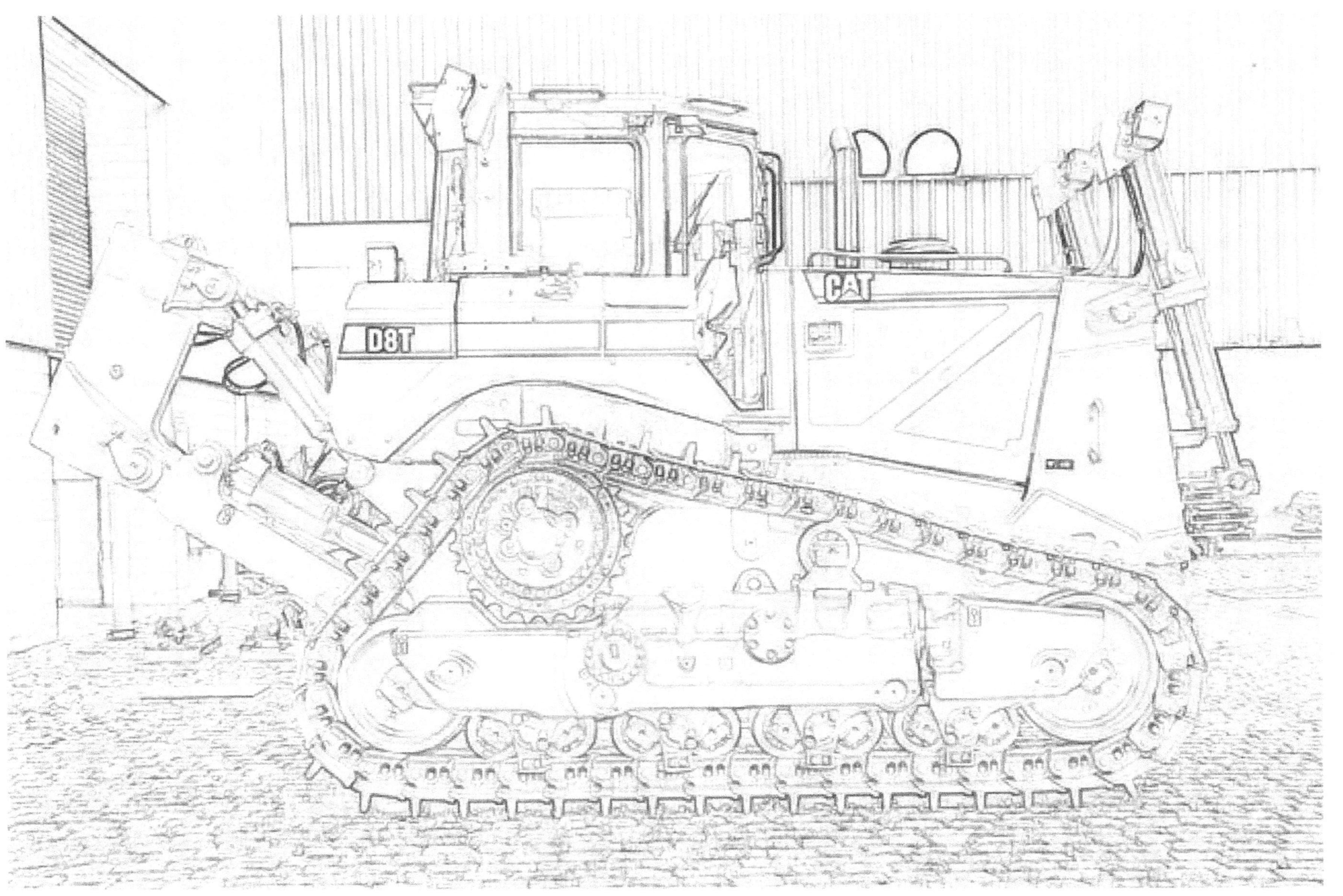
D8T
CAT

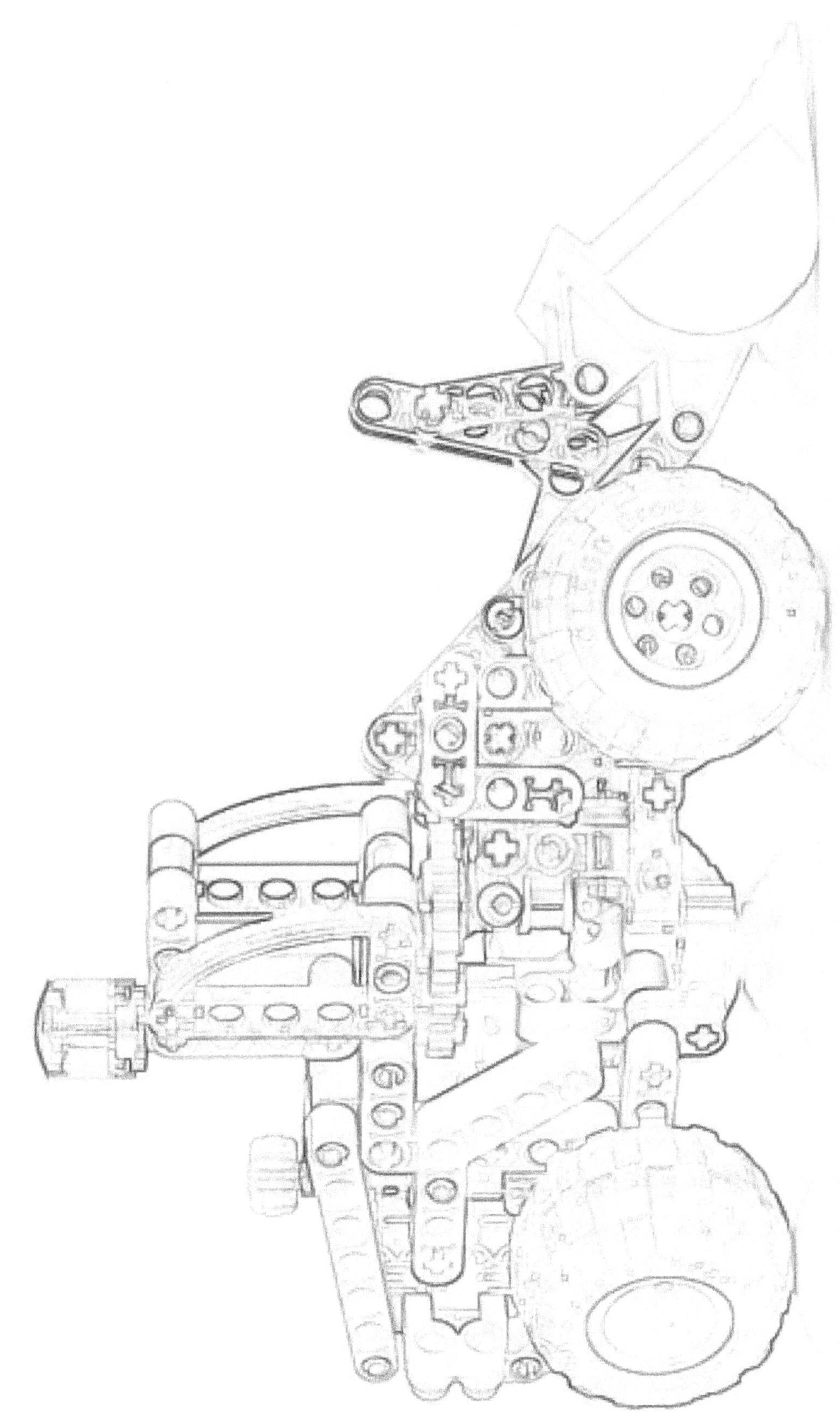

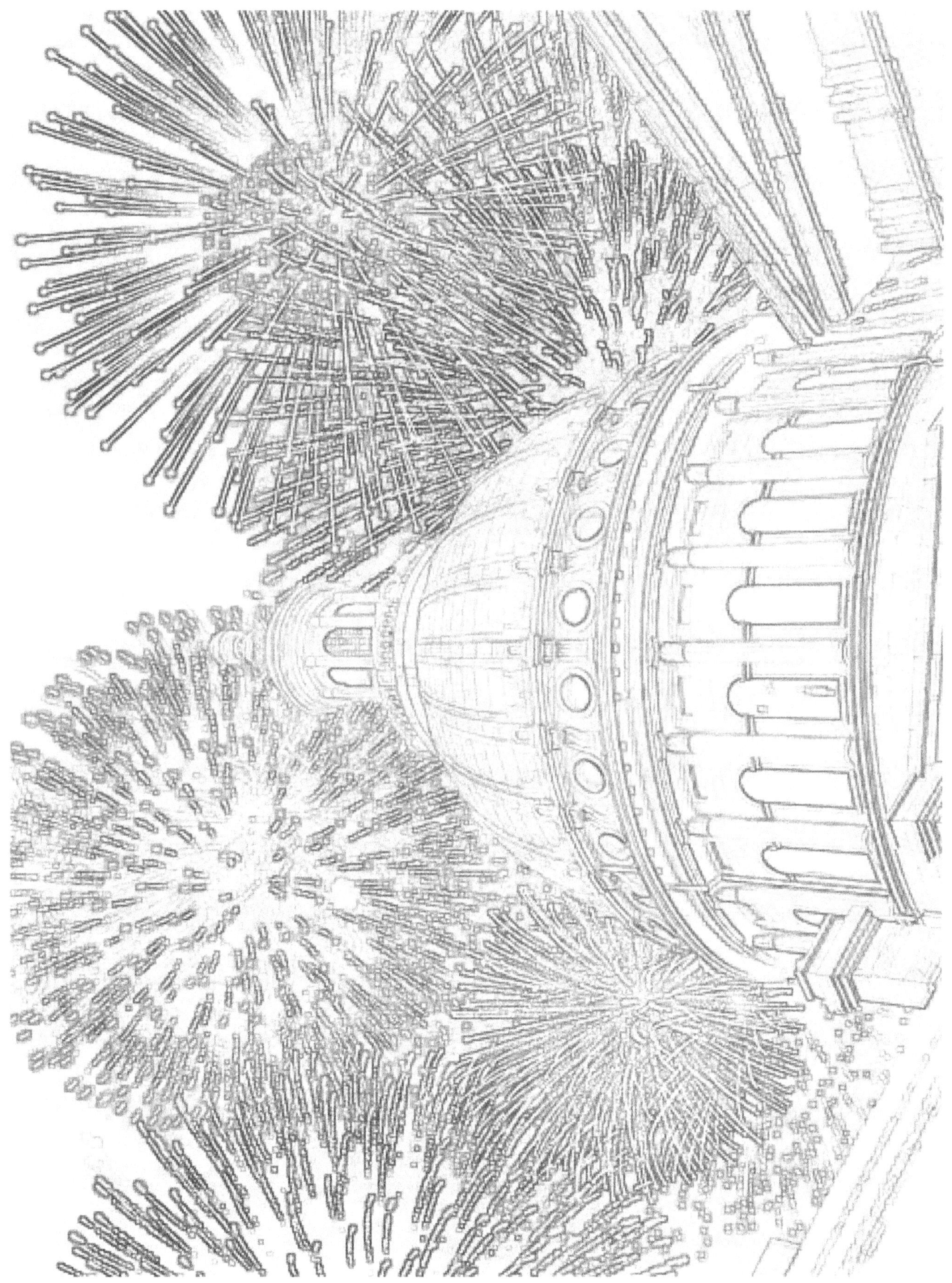

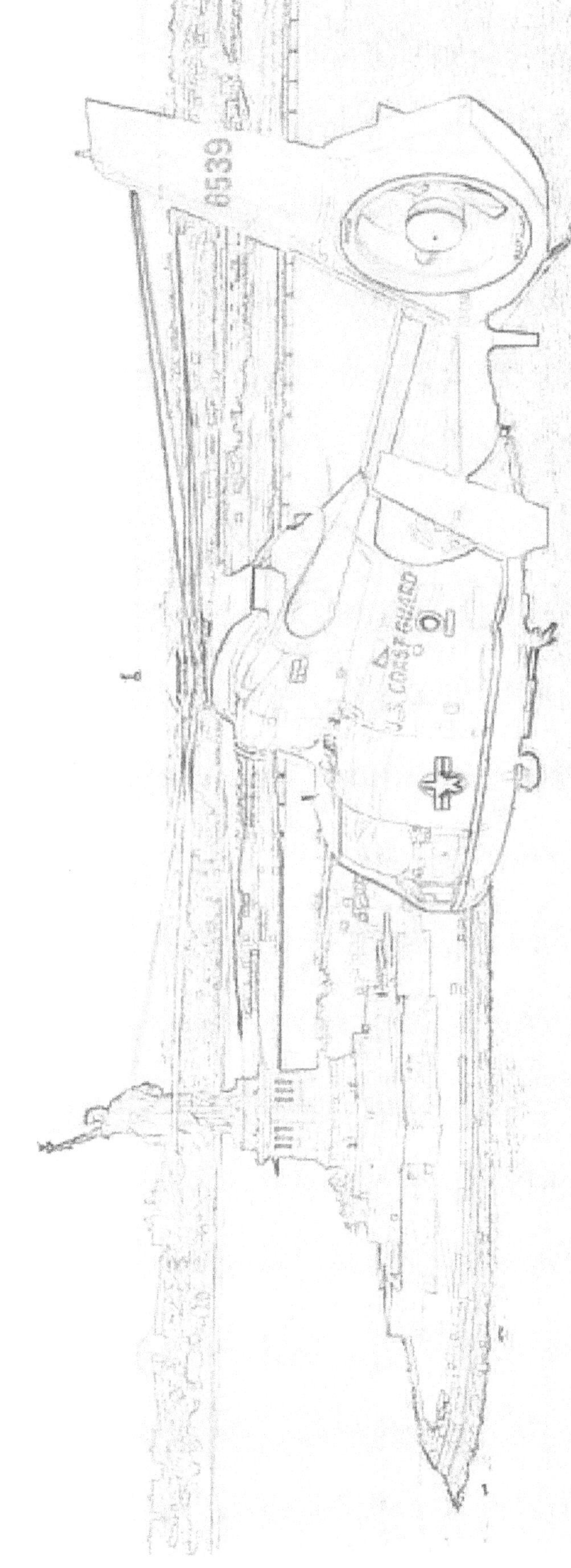
U.S. COAST GUARD
6539

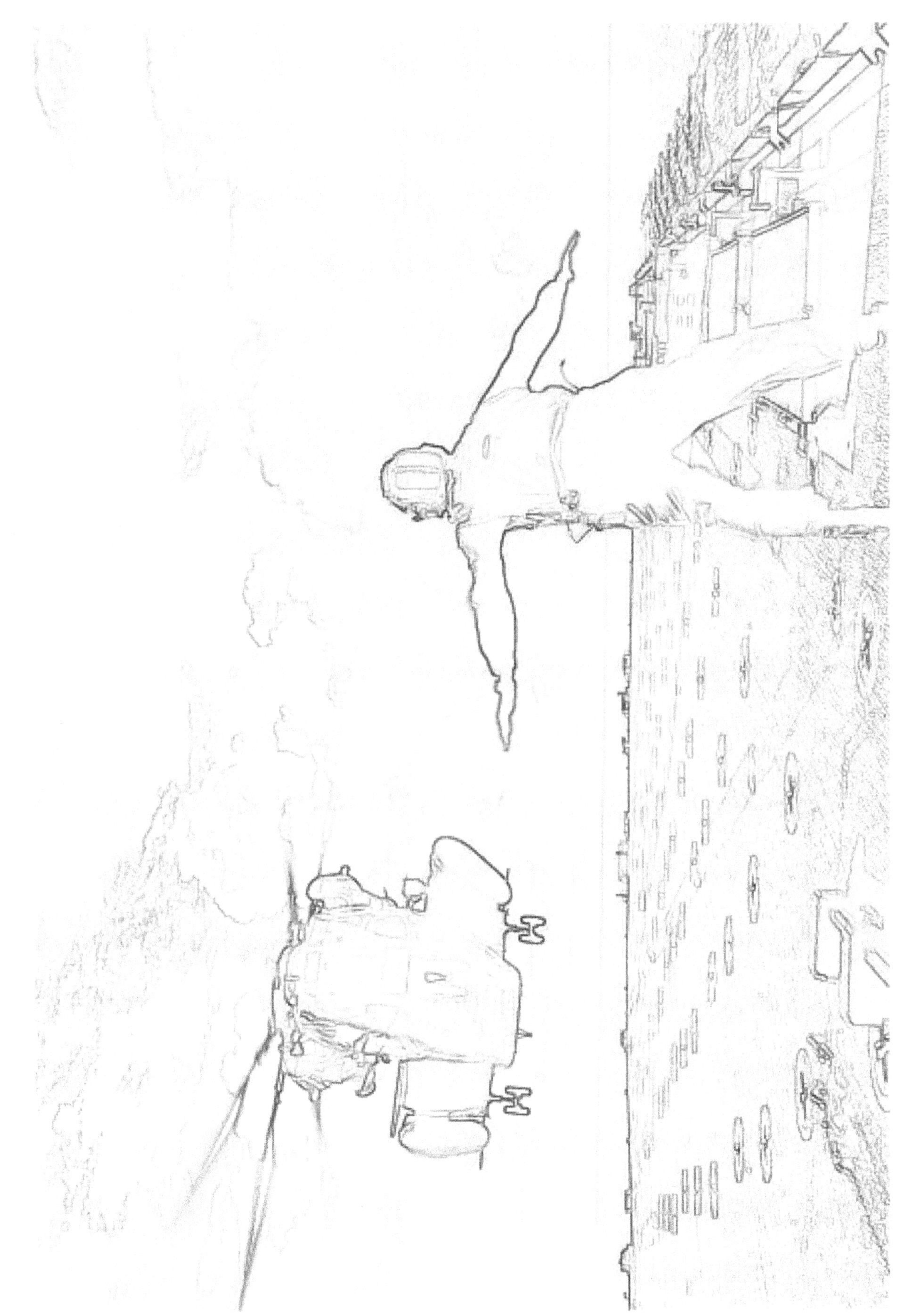

www.ingramcontent.com/pod-product-compliance
Lightning Source LLC
LaVergne TN
LVHW081634120826
845149LV00025B/1912
* 9 7 8 0 9 9 6 5 4 9 9 9 8 *